LINDA WEAVER

PICK A HOUSE AND FLIP IT
Finding Real Estate Investments

Copyright © 2024 by Linda Weaver

All rights reserved. No part of this publication may be reproduced, stored or transmitted in any form or by any means, electronic, mechanical, photocopying, recording, scanning, or otherwise without written permission from the publisher. It is illegal to copy this book, post it to a website, or distribute it by any other means without permission.

Linda Weaver asserts the moral right to be identified as the author of this work.

Linda Weaver has no responsibility for the persistence or accuracy of URLs for external or third-party Internet Websites referred to in this publication and does not guarantee that any content on such Websites is, or will remain, accurate or appropriate.

Designations used by companies to distinguish their products are often claimed as trademarks. All brand names and product names used in this book and on its cover are trade names, service marks, trademarks and registered trademarks of their respective owners. The publishers and the book are not associated with any product or vendor mentioned in this book. None of the companies referenced within the book have endorsed the book.

First edition

This book was professionally typeset on Reedsy.
Find out more at reedsy.com

Contents

	Introduction	1
1	Establish a Network	3
2	Market Research	5
3	Location, Location, Location	8
4	Inspect the Property	11
5	Cosmetics	14
6	Structure	16
7	Estimate Renovation Costs	20
8	Conclusion	24
9	Resources	26

Introduction

This book will walk you through the process of finding a house to renovate and flip. Finding the right house to flip takes time but is worth the research and waiting. Selecting the right property is an important key to successfully investing in real estate. There will be many houses to choose from to flip but you need the tools to narrow down the most profitable deal. If your initial cost of purchasing the property is too high, it will be way more difficult to generate a profit after renovating and selling. If you overpay for the house initially, it will be very difficult to generate a profit after renovation costs. Researching houses to find which is the lowest initial investment for the highest return of profit is the goal. Homework is required to determine which property has the most potential for profit.

My interest in the topic began at an early age. I would spend hours driving around looking for properties that were in need of repair. If it wasn't listed for sale, I would look up the property owner through the real estate website. It was so exciting to finally buy a house and start working on it. I happened to marry a guy that was incredibly handy and could fix nearly any issue we ran into when renovating. Cosmetic repairs were more easily tackled, but some renovations needed contractor assistance. We did run into properties that required permits for repairs such as septic tanks, drain fields, plumbing, electric and HVAC. In those cases, we gathered the most cost effective bid and hired the work to be done. You can find profitable investments whether you plan to do work yourself or contract it out. The trick is taking the cost for each specific investment and determining if the numbers work resulting in the desired profit. If they don't, then pass on the purchase.

There are many myths that characterize renovating investment properties as an easy project. However, the process of finding, evaluating, renovating and selling the properties is quite difficult, requiring a great deal of market awareness as well as skill to perform the required renovations. When looking for a profitable house flip, it is important to know that it will take time and a significant amount of research. Investors that are planning to renovate a house for profit, but lack the skill to perform a majority if not all of the work themselves are in for a big surprise. These investors will need to contract the work out which can make the overall investment cost prohibitive, so the property has to be bought at a price that takes those costs into consideration.

You may run across the occasional investment that can be acquired at such a low price and in need of such minor repair skill, but these are few and far between. This is why it is important to evaluate each project on an individual basis to analyze potential profitability in order to avoid surprises. The return on investment (ROI) is determined by the purchase price, renovation costs and sale price. You need to know your ROI range before making a purchase.

The most important first step in pursuing a house to flip is knowing where to start and actually starting. Real estate investment dreams and goals are only just that until you put in the effort to make them a reality.

1

Establish a Network

Find a Real Estate Agent

First, find a qualified local real estate agent that can guide you in your house flip search. The initial homework is a key in finding profitable investment properties. One of the most important steps in this initial phase of investing in renovation real estate is to establish a network of individuals to help you search for that investment. Become acquainted with a qualified, local real estate agent that is familiar with the community and market. This agent should have access to data of sales trend analysis for the area you are targeting for investment and help you pursue or eliminate potential projects.

Alert Personal Network

It is also important to put the word out to friends, family and co-workers about the type of house you are looking for which is basically properties that are in need of repair. Word of mouth is a powerful tool and can provide leads to houses that may not even be on the market. It could be a friend of a friend who knows someone that is selling a house that has been in the family for years and is run down. Sometimes people inherit property that they don't want, and they just want a quick sale without the hassle of doing any repairs. There are so many possibilities with your personal network so be sure to get the word out. In addition to searching for properties in your personal network, it is important to research local and online sources as well as a qualified real estate agent to aid with your search.

Find a Lender

In order to acquire a house to flip, you must secure funding or pay cash. If you have cash to fund your project, that is fantastic but most investors start with securing a loan. Find a lender for your project. Lenders offer many types of loans that can help get you started in your house flipping journey. If you already own a home, a home equity line of credit (HELOC) is an option. With a HELOC, you can borrow against equity you already have in an existing property to fund the purchase of another. A conventional loan is another option. A 15-30 year fixed rate mortgage with no prepayment penalties is another way to fund your project. Speak with a qualified lender to determine your options and your comfortable threshold amount to borrow.

2

Market Research

The initial investigation also covers extracting items such as price, square footage, number of bedrooms and bathrooms and general condition of the house and comparing it with others like it in the market area. This information can be obtained from your local real estate agent via data from the Multiple Listing Service (MLS). As you learn how your agent searches for properties, you can apply that knowledge to your own searches on public platforms such as zillow and realtor.com for example.

Perform a market analysis of the area you are targeting. Ask your real estate agent to research sales, pending sales, expired listings and existing listings for the area. You can extract a market trend from this data and be better equipped to analyze potential renovation property. Periodically, research and document this information in order to evaluate the movement of market conditions. Remember the market is ever changing and what was evident in the market six months ago may not be evident today.

In addition, it is important to evaluate market economy as part of the overall market analysis to give insight into future market developments.

Research Local and Online Sources

Zillow is an easy way to keep an eye on your target market. You can limit your search to include price, square footage, type of home, lot size, and location etc. Key words like "investment", "repair", "opportunity", "tear down", "renovate", "TLC", "as-is", "fixer upper", "needs work" can help narrow your search to homes needing repairs. HUD is another source of homes available for sale that may need repair and may be distressed foreclosures. Realtor.com and auctions.com also provide insight to available properties.

Drive Drive Drive

The best way to visually see potential real estate investments is to drive, drive, drive. Driving through neighborhoods visually shows you the condition of the homes in the area and gives you a feel for the neighborhood atmosphere. Neighborhoods with large mature trees give a warmer feeling than those with little or no mature trees. You are looking for a home that doesn't quite fit into the neighborhood. Look for the home that needs paint, the shades are pulled, looks vacant, grass is tall etc. An unmaintained house is a sign of a potential motivated seller. This is the house to research. If you see someone walking their dog, ask if they know of anyone interested in selling in the neighborhood. This is a great way to get market information from boots on the ground.

Driving through a neighborhood once is not enough. It is important to consistently drive through and visit the neighborhoods you are targeting so you don't miss a deal.

Monitoring these target neighborhoods also gives you insight to who

MARKET RESEARCH

your potential buyers will be based on who is living in the neighborhood.

3

Location, Location, Location

You have probably heard the saying that location, location, location means everything when investing in property. Well, this saying is most often true. Location is the key to successfully investing in real estate renovations. Just because you can buy a house at a price significantly lower than market value which has great potential for renovation doesn't necessarily mean it will be a successful investment solely based on its location. For example, let's say that you purchase this "great deal" and renovate it, however, the location is known for slow sales and lack of significant appeal to a majority of homebuyers. You may wait for a significant period of time before you have an opportunity to sell and then, the price offered may be significantly below what you expected due solely to location. Given the importance of location, let's evaluate the characteristics that help you determine the desirability of a location you choose to target. Location desirability creates profit. If the location of a house is desirable to a majority of homebuyers more than likely you will be able to sell it in a reasonable time for a reasonable price in various market conditions. A prudent investor must carefully select property that is most likely to sell whenever it is placed on the market and can be counted on to attract homebuyers under a variety of market conditions. Query your real estate agent as to the desirability of the location of the house. The agent can tell you how many listings have become available in the market in the last thirty days and which ones have sold and at what price. This will give you an idea of how fast or slow the market is moving in this location and what the comparable house sales have been recently.

Learn the Neighborhood

Items that detract or attribute to the desirability of a house and location are the neighborhood and lot. Conduct a neighborhood analysis for its location to schools, churches, hospitals, shopping malls, parks, etc. In addition, analyze the exposure to busy vs. quiet streets within the surrounding neighborhood which can affect the overall value of the investment property. The neighborhood should be evaluated by comparing the sizes and conditions of houses in the area. If all of the houses are generally comparable then it will be easier to determine market value. However, if the houses vary significantly in size and condition, then it will be more difficult to determine the potential market value for your particular investment once renovated. Inquire with your local real estate agent whether or not the location and neighborhood is consistent in sales, is on the uphill climb, or continues to decline. If the neighborhood is on a downhill turn and is continuing to demand lower and lower sales prices, then it would be wise to pass up any properties in the area.

When targeting areas to invest in, keep in mind that middle class neighborhoods have the most consistent sales in all types of market conditions. This is primarily because the middle class has the greatest number of future buyers when it is time to sell that renovated house.

In addition, when evaluating a neighborhood, you need to see if there is anything nearby that would detract from the value of the subject property. For example, do neighbors keep their yard mowed and picked up, are there any run down houses that detract from the value of others, is there a railroad track nearby, or do you hear airplane or highway traffic. It is important to learn the demographics to better know what your target market can be. Not only is the neighborhood important but the lot is important as well.

4

Inspect the Property

Curb Appeal

Initial visual inspection of the property will help determine what repairs are necessary and what changes can be made to increase the marketability of the house. Evaluate the foundation of the house. Look for problem areas that may need repair such as cracks, leaks in the basement, damage to foundation walls, etc. A crack in the foundation wall can mean anything from a stress crack that can be fixed for a reasonable price to a bow in the basement wall that will require significant investment to correct. The foundation is the basis upon which the house is built upon, therefore, it must be evaluated for required repairs. A building inspector can assist you with this evaluation and is more highly qualified to thoroughly inspect every aspect of the house (roof, foundation, electric, plumbing, HVAC etc).

Floor Plan Functionality

Evaluate the floor plan of the house for functionality. It is important that the floor plan has a functional flow to it. Some older house floor plans are chopped up and don't have an open flow to them. Your first impression of the floor plan is normally right. If you walk into a house and the layout of the rooms doesn't seem quite right, it probably isn't. You need to approach the house as if you were the potential buyer after renovation. If the house has only one bathroom but four bedrooms, this will detract from the functionality of the floor plan. However, in some instances the floor plan can be altered to make it more functional. Ask yourself which attributes would you be looking for as a homebuyer. For example, if there is limited wall space in the room due to multiple entrances, eliminate one of them. If there is only one bath in the house, look for a place to add another. If there is no main floor laundry, evaluate where a laundry room can be added or what existing space can be utilized for one. If the kitchen is dark, drab and closed in, evaluate the structure of the ceiling to see if it can be vaulted and if windows can be added for lighting.

It may not be wise to purchase a house that can't be altered to satisfy a majority of homebuyers needs. For example, it is hard to change a floor plan that is not open and doesn't flow well for daily use. Only make alterations that improve the flow and value of the house. Some alterations can actually make the house dysfunctional. For example, adding french doors to the kitchen may sound like a great idea, but the doors open too far into the usable space of the kitchen and make it appear smaller and less usable. Adding an island in the kitchen may take up too much floor space making it difficult to place furniture. Try to determine possibilities of making the house more functional for daily living with every improvement you consider making.

Evaluate the lot to see if there is proper drainage, even elevation, etc. Check with local zoning to see if the lot is in the flood plain or has

INSPECT THE PROPERTY

any specific restrictions. Evaluate the attractiveness of the lot such as mature trees and room for family activities in the backyard. A fence would be appealing to families with children and would further expand your potential buyer pool.

Evaluate whether or not the yard has the potential of being an attractive yard which can increase the salability of the investment property. Some yards will be significantly run down and neglected. However, most yards can often be cured with a little maintenance, landscaping and tender loving care.

Lot size is another key factor to consider. Generally, a larger lot is more appealing to most potential buyers. Evaluate the lot size to those in the neighborhood to see how it compares in similarity. I wouldn't buy the house with the smallest lot in the neighborhood unless it was an incredible deal. You will be competing with houses with larger lots when selling and will likely experience a price adjustment due to your smaller lot.

Outdoor spaces are becoming increasingly popular. Creating a private backyard space with fencing and landscaping can greatly enhance the potential success of your house flip.

5

Cosmetics

Finishes

Floor finishes consist of carpet, vinyl, tile, wood floors, marble etc. If these items are in good condition but are not in style, they will need to be replaced to appeal to the average homebuyer.

Kitchen

Kitchen appliances such as dishwasher, microwave, oven and refrigerator should all match and be in good working condition. An update to these items may be necessary depending upon the price point of the house. The condition of the kitchen is critical for homebuyers since so much time is spent in the kitchen and it is such a focal point in the house.

Extras

COSMETICS

Extra amenities such as fireplaces, decks and fencing add to the value of the house and should be checked for functionality. Decks and fencing conditions, quality and workmanship should be checked. These items can easily be refreshed with power washing but may need wood rot repair etc which is more costly.

Exterior

The exterior appearance of the house is the first thing buyers see so its condition is critical in order to get them inside the door to take a look for purchase. Evaluate the condition for obvious repairs. Brick may need to have tuckpointing repairs, window frames may need painting, siding may need to be replaced in areas, or the entire exterior may need a fresh coat of paint etc. Remember, if the house is not attractive from the outside, it will be hard to convince buyers to come inside. It won't sell if you can't get them in the door.

Interior

The interior appearance of the house must be appealing to the average homebuyer. Anything too modern or too traditional will only appeal to a specific segment of the market and will limit your buyer pool. Any paint or wall paper should be somewhat neutral or removed. This is where creativity and taste come into play. Your goal is to decorate the house in a way that enables it to be desirable to a majority of homebuyers. The key is to avoid extremes because this will limit your homebuyer pool. If you need help with this, research sold properties to determine what style is getting the highest price per square foot.

6

Structure

Framing

The framing of the house is known as the skeleton of the house and must be checked as well for any needed repairs. The main problem to look for would be faulty construction. For example, an individual may have attempted to renovate the house and in the process removed a supporting wall in order to extend a room. If this was done improperly, the structure of the framing may have been weakened. Also, evaluate whether the house has had previous or existing termite damage. Termite damage can affect the structural integrity of the house. If you are unable to evaluate these items, a termite inspector can assist you and provide a remedy plan if necessary.

Floors

Floors are another area to check for stability in the house structure. Flooring consists of floor joist which has plywood installed on top of it. Things to look for and evaluate are as follows: abnormal vibrations, squeaks, levelness or warping. Abnormal vibrations, for example, when you walk across it may suggest a structural problem with the floor. Squeaks in the floor here and there are not cause for alarm. If squeaks are accompanied by other signs such as a crack in the foundation, floors which literally give up and down when walking across them, then you will want to further investigate. It may be possible to visually see the underneath side of the flooring from the basement ceiling. Look for signs of past water damage especially in wood floors. This will be evidenced by warping such as planks that have raised edges or are bowed in the middle. Water damaged floors can also be uneven and this can be checked with a carpenter's level. If it appears water damage has occurred, it would be wise to check possible plumbing leaks in that area such as a leaking refrigerator, broken pipes, etc. Another reason for a floor to be unlevel is the way it was constructed. Every piece of lumber has a crown. The crown can be a slight to very noticeable rise in the wood. When the house was constructed, the crown of the wood should have been placed upward to take on the weight. When this is not done, problems can occur. An excessive crown can cause a bump in the floor and if placed downward can cause a dip in the floor. Either way, the particular piece of wood should not have been used and correction may require replacement. Another construction issue could be that the joists are not level. These items can also be investigated by a building inspector.

Roof

The roof is another area to evaluate. When scrutinizing the roof, look for any indicated uneven appearances. Sagging between rafters could mean warped or rotten decking. If you see any signs of a roofing problem, investigate the roof through the attic or scuttle of the house to better understand the actual cause of the problem. In some cases, the house may require a new roof. A new roof could mean shingle replacement or the replacement of the plywood underneath. Both can be expensive. A building inspector should be able to direct you to the condition of the roof. A roofing contractor will also be able to inspect, provide scope of repairs needed and provide an estimate to fix it.

Doors and Windows

Doors and windows should be checked for efficiency and functionality. A properly installed door will have even margins at the top, sides and bottom. Open and close the door to see if it works easily or hits the floor or framing at some point during use. As well, open and close the windows to see if they operate properly. Windows also need to be evaluated for efficiency, damage, screens and insulation. Functional problems with doors and windows are generally caused by poor construction, settling or age.

Plumbing, Electrical and HVAC

Plumbing, electrical, and heating and cooling systems should be evaluated to ensure they are in proper working order. Check the faucets and toilets to evaluate water pressure and leaks. Also, check to see if the hot water is hot enough or is scalding hot. If it's not hot enough check the setting on the hot water heater to see if it can be turned up. If it is scalding hot it may indicate that it has sediment at the bottom of the tank or the elements are going bad. Verify that the hot water heater size meets the needs of the size of the house. A building inspector can assist with these evaluations.

Interior Walls

STRUCTURE

Evaluate the interior walls and ceilings for type and condition. More than likely they are either drywall or plaster (found in older homes). Look for cracks, stains, etc. Cracks can be caused from settlement or water damage. Stains indicate water damage so the source needs to be investigated. For example, if you see a crack and stain in the ceiling more than likely there is a bathroom above that has had or currently has a plumbing leak.

7

Estimate Renovation Costs

Evaluate and estimate all renovation costs for necessity. Don't make renovations that are unnecessary and cost prohibitive. When evaluating the market of a given area, you will be able to determine what a totally renovated house will bring in price. Making unnecessary changes and alterations will not necessarily add to what you can ask for the house. Over improvements above the norm in the neighborhood can drive your cost above market performance. You can't expect your house to bring much more than the market norm for the area. This only happens rarely and shouldn't be characterized as typical. You can only stretch your investment intuition so far. The rest must be based on concrete facts about the house and the market. Your real estate agent can also guide you in what repairs will offer the highest return when selling.

In order to determine if a house can be renovated for profit, you need to evaluate all costs associated with the investment. Evaluate the price of the house in comparison with others similar in the area which have already been renovated or are still in good condition. This, in conjunction with a market analysis, can give you an idea of what the renovated house will bring once completed. Again, a real estate agent familiar with the area can estimate what the house could be worth once renovated through market analysis and recent sales, pending sales, listings and expired listings. Next evaluate only necessary renovation expenses. The analysis of renovation cost must be carefully evaluated for accuracy. Additional costs not associated with the renovation must be included in your overall investment analysis such as interest carry. If any loans are being made for the purchase and/or repairs, you must include the cost related to these loans. During the renovations, the house must be insured, therefore, estimate the insurance premium costs during the timeframe you expect to own the house. Once the house is listed for sale, estimate the cost of commission and closing. Consider tax implications such as capital gains taxes. The profit you are expecting to make in conjunction with the risk you are willing to take will help determine whether or not to invest in the project.

Evaluate the sale price of the house to others in the area. In order for you to make money on renovation investments, the house must be purchased at a significantly lower price than other houses in the neighborhood. If you pay market price and then have to invest additionally in renovation costs, you will have invested more than you can sell it for. The purchase price plus renovation costs combined must be a certain percentage below the potential sale price. This percentage depends on how much profit the investor believes is enough to constitute a worthwhile investment. For example, if the purchase price is 100,000, the renovation expenses are 50,000 and the anticipated market value once renovated is 200,000 then you have to decide if this is enough profit to do the deal. It is up to each investor to determine how much profit is enough to justify the cost, time and effort (less taxes, insurance, real estate fee, permits, closing costs, etc.) to justify the investment.

Once the house price is determined, evaluate the house with comparable houses in the area for what it will be worth once renovated. Ask your real estate agent what houses of comparable size are selling for in the area which are either in good condition or already renovated. This comparison will be made to what the real estate agent believes this particular house will bring once renovated according to others like it in the area. Apply the 70 % Rule. Generally speaking you should pay not more than 70% of the house value after renovation less the cost of repairs to renovate the house.

If the house calculates the desired return on investment, then it is time to make an offer, purchase the house and begin repairs. Congratulations, you are on your way to beginning your house flip.

Checklist to consider when buying a house to flip:

- Find a qualified real estate agent
- Put the word out to your personal and professional network
- Perform market research
- Research Local and Online Sources
- Drive Drive Drive
- Location Location Location
- Conduct a neighborhood analysis
- Curb Appeal
- Evaluate the floor plan of the house for functionality
- Evaluate the lot for drainage, restrictions and appeal
- Check out the cosmetics
- Floor finishes
- Kitchen appliances
- Extra amenities
- Exterior appearance
- Interior appearance

ESTIMATE RENOVATION COSTS

- Framing condition
- Floor condition
- Roof Condition
- Door and window functionality
- Plumbing, electrical, and heating and cooling systems should be evaluated to ensure they are in proper working order.
- Evaluate the interior walls and ceilings for type and condition
- Estimate Rehab Costs
- Determine what you can pay in order to make the desired profit after rehab costs
- 70% Rule
- Purchase the house and begin

8

Conclusion

Investing in renovation real estate is an exciting venture. Finding the right house to renovate and flip is an important key to a profitable investment. Your return on investment (ROI) evaluation will vary on each potential flip and needs to be thoroughly evaluated before making a purchase. If you are new to real estate investing, remember to start small. If a small investment has unexpected costs, the impact will be less than if you have a huge project which could lead to huge losses. Be conservative and pick the safest investment. Network with a local real estate agent to help you learn the market and how to find profitable investment property. A seasoned agent can lead you in the right direction as you develop your knowledge of picking the right property. Once you begin to know specific markets you can track opportunities with online search platforms on your own. Driving through neighborhoods helps you learn the area and find visible distressed properties. Finding a house that has the potential to have great curb appeal is the target property. Once you have narrowed down your search, take a physical look at the house. The yard and first appearance of the house is the first impression for homebuyers. Cleaning up debris, landscaping, and painting can make a

CONCLUSION

huge difference to improve curb appeal and ultimately get your potential buyer in the door. If the floorplan doesn't flow well or if you can't make changes to make it better, then it may be best to pass on the deal. Inspect the structure and mechanics of the house to avoid surprises. Determine if the house only requires a cosmetic fix that you can self perform or will it require more significant repairs that you will be hiring contractors to perform. The easiest flip involves painting, replacing hardware and updating landscaping. These simple updates can greatly improve the value. Evaluate the project costs to determine if this is a profitable deal. If the house passes the profitability test, buy it and begin the renovation. Good luck and enjoy searching for a house to flip.

Please leave a positive review for the book on Amazon, if you found the book to be helpful in your search for a house flip.

9

Resources

Arthur, M. (2023b, October 25). *How to find, afford and improve a Fixer-Upper.* Zillow. https://zillow.com/learn/buying-a-fixer-upper/
How to find houses to flip | Flipping Houses 101. (2022, July 20). Rehab Financial | Private Money Lender.

10 Outdoor projects to focus on as a flipper to maximize ROI. (n.d.). https://www.propstream.com/real-estate-investor-blog/10-outdoor-projects-to-focus-on-as-a-flipper-to-maximize-roi

What is the 70% rule in house flipping? (n.d.). Rocket Mortgage. https://www.rocketmortgage.com/learn/what-is-70-rule-in-house-flipping#:~:text=The%2070%25%20rule%20helps%20home,costs%20of%20renovating%20the%20property.

Foreclosure homes. (n.d.). https://www.hudhomesusa.org/landing.html?adid=HHU2959011&AFID=flip%20houses%20for%20sale&XID=Cj0K

RESOURCES

CQjw4Oe4BhCcARIsADQ0csnr_6MX4l83_Pia3lnQGVck9LHbfbZUj46NOIMt8YvWxRh6-w5ktNEaAuFAEALw_wcB&gad_source=1&gclid=Cj0KCQjw4Oe4BhCcARIsADQ0csnr_6MX4l83_Pia3lnQGVck9LHbfbZUj46NOIMt8YvWxRh6-w5ktNEaAuFAEALw_wcB

Woodman, C. (2023, November 15). How to get a loan to flip a house - New Silver. *New Silver.* https://newsilver.com/the-lender/how-to-get-a-loan-to-flip-a-house/

www.ingramcontent.com/pod-product-compliance
Lightning Source LLC
Chambersburg PA
CBHW030045230526
45472CB00005B/1679